HATCHET

A guide for the novel by Gary Paulsen
Great Works Author: Suzanne Barchers

Publishing Credits

Jill K. Mulhall, M.Ed., *Editor*

Image Credits

Alin Brotea—Shutterstock (cover); All other images Shutterstock

Standards

© 2007 Teachers of English to Speakers of Other Languages, Inc. (TESOL)
© 2007 Board of Regents of the University of Wisconsin System. World-Class Instructional Design and Assessment (WIDA)
© Copyright 2010. National Governors Association Center for Best Practices and Council of Chief State School Officers.
All rights reserved.

Shell Education

5301 Oceanus Drive
Huntington Beach, CA 92649-1030
http://www.shelleducation.com

ISBN 978-1-4258-8979-1
© 2014 Shell Educational Publishing, Inc.

Table of Contents

How to Use This Literature Guide

Today's standards demand rigor and relevance in the reading of complex texts. The units in this series guide teachers in a rich and deep exploration of worthwhile works of literature for classroom study. The most rigorous instruction can also be interesting and engaging!

Many current strategies for effective literacy instruction have been incorporated into these instructional guides for literature. Throughout the units, text-dependent questions are used to determine comprehension of the book as well as student interpretation of the vocabulary words. The books chosen for the series are complex exemplars of carefully crafted works of literature. Close reading is used throughout the units to guide students toward revisiting the text and using textual evidence to respond to prompts orally and in writing. Students must analyze the story elements in multiple assignments for each section of the book. All of these strategies work together to rigorously guide students through their study of literature.

The next few pages will make clear how to use this guide for a purposeful and meaningful literature study. Each section of this guide is set up in the same way to make it easier for you to implement the instruction in your classroom.

Theme Thoughts

The great works of literature used throughout this series have important themes that have been relevant to people for many years. Many of the themes will be discussed during the various sections of this instructional guide. However, it would also benefit students to have independent time to think about the key themes of the novel.

Before students begin reading, have them complete *Pre-Reading Theme Thoughts* (page 13). This graphic organizer will allow students to think about the themes outside the context of the story. They'll have the opportunity to evaluate statements based on important themes and defend their opinions. Be sure to have students keep their papers for comparison to the *Post-Reading Theme Thoughts* (page 64). This graphic organizer is similar to the pre-reading activity. However, this time, students will be answering the questions from the point of view of one of the characters of the novel. They have to think about how the character would feel about each statement and defend their thoughts. To conclude the activity, have students compare what they thought about the themes before they read the novel to what the characters discovered during the story.

How to Use This Literature Guide (cont.)

Vocabulary

Each teacher overview page has definitions and sentences about how key vocabulary words are used in the section. These words should be introduced and discussed with students. There are two student vocabulary activity pages in each section. On the first page, students are asked to define the ten words chosen by the author of this unit. On the second page in most sections, each student will select at least eight words that he or she finds interesting or difficult. For each section, choose one of these pages for your students to complete. With either assignment, you may want to have students get into pairs to discuss the meanings of the words. Allow students to use reference guides to define the words. Monitor students to make sure the definitions they have found are accurate and relate to how the words are used in the text.

On some of the vocabulary student pages, students are asked to answer text-related questions about the vocabulary words. The following question stems will help you create your own vocabulary questions if you'd like to extend the discussion.

- How does this word describe _____'s character?
- In what ways does this word relate to the problem in this story?
- How does this word help you understand the setting?
- In what ways is this word related to the story's solution?
- Describe how this word supports the novel's theme of . . . .
- What visual images does this word bring to your mind?
- For what reasons might the author have chosen to use this particular word?

At times, more work with the words will help students understand their meanings. The following quick vocabulary activities are a good way to further study the words.

- Have students practice their vocabulary and writing skills by creating sentences and/or paragraphs in which multiple vocabulary words are used correctly and with evidence of understanding.
- Students can play vocabulary concentration. Students make a set of cards with the words and a separate set of cards with the definitions. Then, students lay the cards out on the table and play concentration. The goal of the game is to match vocabulary words with their definitions.
- Students can create word journal entries about the words. Students choose words they think are important and then describe why they think each word is important within the novel.

How to Use This Literature Guide (cont.)

Analyzing the Literature

After students have read each section, hold small-group or whole-class discussions. Questions are written at two levels of complexity to allow you to decide which questions best meet the needs of your students. The Level 1 questions are typically less abstract than the Level 2 questions. Level 1 is indicated by a square, while Level 2 is indicated by a triangle. These questions focus on the various story elements, such as character, setting, and plot. Student pages are provided if you want to assign these questions for individual student work before your group discussion. Be sure to add further questions as your students discuss what they've read. For each question, a few key points are provided for your reference as you discuss the novel with students.

Reader Response

In today's classrooms, there are often great readers who are below average writers. So much time and energy is spent in classrooms getting students to read on grade level, that little time is left to focus on writing skills. To help teachers include more writing in their daily literacy instruction, each section of this guide has a literature-based reader response prompt. Each of the three genres of writing is used in the reader responses within this guide: narrative, informative/explanatory, and argument. Students have a choice between two prompts for each reader response. One response requires students to make connections between the reading and their own lives. The other prompt requires students to determine text-to-text connections or connections within the text.

Close Reading the Literature

Within each section, students are asked to closely reread a short section of text. Since some versions of the novels have different page numbers, the selections are described by chapter and location, along with quotations to guide the readers. After each close reading, there are text-dependent questions to be answered by students.

Encourage students to read each question one at a time and then go back to the text and discover the answer. Work with students to ensure that they use the text to determine their answers rather than making unsupported inferences. Once students have answered the questions, discuss what they discovered. Suggested answers are provided in the answer key.

How to Use This Literature Guide (cont.)

Close Reading the Literature (cont.)

The generic, open-ended stems below can be used to write your own text-dependent questions if you would like to give students more practice.

- Give evidence from the text to support . . . .
- Justify your thinking using text evidence about . . . .
- Find evidence to support your conclusions about . . . .
- What text evidence helps the reader understand . . . ?
- Use the book to tell why _____ happens.
- Based on events in the story, ...
- Use text evidence to describe why . . . .

Making Connections

The activities in this section help students make cross-curricular connections to writing, mathematics, science, social studies, or the fine arts. Each of these types of activities requires higher-order thinking skills from students.

Creating with the Story Elements

It is important to spend time discussing the common story elements in literature. Understanding the characters, setting, and plot can increase students' comprehension and appreciation of the story. If teachers discuss these elements daily, students will more likely internalize the concepts and look for the elements in their independent reading. Another important reason for focusing on the story elements is that students will be better writers if they think about how the stories they read are constructed.

Students are given three options for working with the story elements. They are asked to create something related to the characters, setting, or plot of the novel. Students are given a choice on this activity so that they can decide to complete the activity that most appeals to them. Different multiple intelligences are used so that the activities are diverse and interesting to all students.

How to Use This Literature Guide *(cont.)*

Culminating Activity

This open-ended, cross-curricular activity requires higher-order thinking and allows for a creative product. Students will enjoy getting the chance to share what they have discovered through reading the novel. Be sure to allow them enough time to complete the activity at school or home.

Comprehension Assessment

The questions in this section are modeled after current standardized tests to help students analyze what they've read and prepare for tests they may see in their classrooms. The questions are dependent on the text and require critical-thinking skills to answer.

Response to Literature

The final post-reading activity is an essay based on the text that also requires further research by students. This is a great way to extend this book into other curricular areas. A suggested rubric is provided for teacher reference.

Correlation to the Standards

Shell Education is committed to producing educational materials that are research and standards based. As part of this effort, we have correlated all of our products to the academic standards of all 50 states, the District of Columbia, the Department of Defense Dependents Schools, and all Canadian provinces.

Purpose and Intent of Standards

Standards are designed to focus instruction and guide adoption of curricula. Standards are statements that describe the criteria necessary for students to meet specific academic goals. They define the knowledge, skills, and content students should acquire at each level. Standards are also used to develop standardized tests to evaluate students' academic progress. Teachers are required to demonstrate how their lessons meet standards. Standards are used in the development of all of our products, so educators can be assured they meet high academic standards.

How to Find Standards Correlations

To print a customized correlation report of this product for your state, visit our website at http://www.shelleducation.com and follow the online directions. If you require assistance in printing correlation reports, please contact our Customer Service Department at 1-877-777-3450.

Correlation to the Standards (cont.)

Standards Correlation Chart

The lessons in this guide were written to support the Common Core College and Career Readiness Anchor Standards. This chart indicates which sections of this guide address the anchor standards.

Common Core College and Career Readiness Anchor Standard	Section
CCSS.ELA-Literacy.CCRA.R.1—Read closely to determine what the text says explicitly and to make logical inferences from it; cite specific textual evidence when writing or speaking to support conclusions drawn from the text.	Close Reading the Literature Sections 1–5; Making Connections Sections 1–3, 5; Creating with the Story Elements Sections 1–5; Culminating Activity
CCSS.ELA-Literacy.CCRA.R.2—Determine central ideas or themes of a text and analyze their development; summarize the key supporting details and ideas.	Analyzing the Literature Sections 1–5; Close Reading the Literature Sections 1–5; Making Connections Sections 2, 4; Creating with the Story Elements Sections 1–3; Culminating Activity; Post-Reading Response to Literature
CCSS.ELA-Literacy.CCRA.R.3—Analyze how and why individuals, events, or ideas develop and interact over the course of a text.	Analyzing the Literature Sections 1-5; Creating with the Story Elements Sections 2, 4
CCSS.ELA-Literacy.CCRA.R.4—Interpret words and phrases as they are used in a text, including determining technical, connotative, and figurative meanings, and analyze how specific word choices shape meaning or tone.	Vocabulary Sections 1–5
CCSS.ELA-Literacy.CCRA.R.5—Analyze the structure of texts, including how specific sentences, paragraphs, and larger portions of the text (e.g., a section, a chapter, a scene, or a stanza) relate to one another and the whole.	Making Connections Section 5; Creating with the Story Elements Sections 2–4
CCSS.ELA-Literacy.CCRA.R.10—Read and comprehend complex literary and informational texts independently and proficiently.	Entire Unit
CCSS.ELA-Literacy.CCRA.W.1—Write arguments to support claims in an analysis of substantive topics or texts, using valid reasoning and relevant and sufficient evidence.	Reader Response Sections 2–5
CCSS.ELA-Literacy.CCRA.W.2—Write informative/explanatory texts to examine and convey complex ideas and information clearly and accurately through the effective selection, organization, and analysis of content.	Readers Response Sections 1, 3; Creating with the Story Elements Sections 4–5; Post-Reading Theme Thoughts; Culminating Activity; Post-Reading Response to Literature
CCSS.ELA-Literacy.CCRA.W.3—Write narratives to develop real or imagined experiences or events using effective technique, well-chosen details, and well-structured event sequences.	Creating with the Story Elements Sections 2–3; Reader Response Sections 1–2, 4–5
CCSS.ELA-Literacy.CCRA.W.4—Produce clear and coherent writing in which the development, organization, and style are appropriate to task, purpose, and audience.	Creating with the Story Elements Sections 2, 4–5; Post-Reading Theme Thoughts; Culminating Activity; Post-Reading Response to Literature

Correlation to the Standards (cont.)

Standards Correlation Chart (cont.)

Common Core College and Career Readiness Anchor Standard	Section
CCSS.ELA-Literacy.CCRA.W.6—Use technology, including the Internet, to produce and publish writing and to interact and collaborate with others.	Making Connections Section 4; Culminating Activity; Post-Reading Response to Literature
CCSS.ELA-Literacy.CCRA.W.9—Draw evidence from literary or informational texts to support analysis, reflection, and research.	Making Connections Sections 2, 4–5; Creating with the Story Elements Sections 2, 4–5; Reader Response Sections 1–5; Culminating Activity; Post-Reading Response to Literature
CCSS.ELA-Literacy.CCRA.L.1—Demonstrate command of the conventions of standard English grammar and usage when writing or speaking.	Reader Response Sections 1–5; Creating with the Story Elements Sections 2, 4–5; Post-Reading Theme Thoughts; Culminating Activity; Post-Reading Response to Literature
CCSS.ELA-Literacy.CCRA.L.4—Determine or clarify the meaning of unknown and multiple-meaning words and phrases by using context clues, analyzing meaningful word parts, and consulting general and specialized reference materials, as appropriate.	Vocabulary Sections 1–5
CCSS.ELA-Literacy.CCRA.L.6—Acquire and use accurately a range of general academic and domain-specific words and phrases sufficient for reading, writing, speaking, and listening at the college and career readiness level; demonstrate independence in gathering vocabulary knowledge when encountering an unknown term important to comprehension or expression.	Vocabulary Sections 1–5

TESOL and WIDA Standards

The lessons in this book promote English language development for English language learners. The following TESOL and WIDA English Language Development Standards are addressed through the activities in this book:

- **Standard 1:** English language learners communicate for social and instructional purposes within the school setting.

- **Standard 2:** English language learners communicate information, ideas and concepts necessary for academic success in the content area of language arts.

About the Author—Gary Paulsen

Born in Minnesota on May 17, 1939, Gary Paulsen credits his grandmothers, his aunts, and a librarian with helping him through early years made difficult by parents who "fought and drank." After being offered a library book, and later a library card, Paulsen escaped his tumultuous home life through reading. Despite his love of books, school was difficult because he was constantly moving; Paulsen never spent more than five months in any school.

Out of necessity, Paulsen was a hard worker from the time he was a teenager, running away to join a carnival at age 14. He held down a variety of odd jobs, served in the army, took correspondence courses, worked in publishing, and eventually turned to writing. He did not achieve instant success as a writer. Relocating to Minnesota with a wife and a son, he lived in a converted chicken coop with no indoor plumbing while he gardened, hunted—and tried to sell articles and books.

Finally, he turned to writing fiction. *The Foxman*, his novel for middle school children, was published in 1977. His books are firmly rooted in reality and his personal experiences, particularly those as an outdoorsman. During his years of living in Minnesota, Paulsen worked with dogs while running traps, and that led him to running the Iditarod Trail Sled Dog Race. Those experiences shaped books such as *Woodsong* (a memoir) and *Dogsong*, a Newbery Honor Book. *Hatchet*, also a Newbery Honor Book, was not published until 1987—and it had been rejected by three publishers. *Hatchet* is considered one of Paulsen's most compelling novels. Paulsen wrote four follow-up books and called the set Brian's Saga. He later wrote about the stories behind the books in *Guts: The True Stories Behind Hatchet and the Brian Books*.

Paulsen has written more than 200 books, hundreds of articles, and numerous short stories. Despite the fame he has achieved, he continues to live simply, dedicating himself to the craft of writing. He is also devoted to reaching his readers, especially those who are struggling to fit in or survive. Like Brian in *Hatchet*, Paulsen says that he is a full-time survivor.

Possible Texts for Text Comparisons

There are four books in the Brian's Saga series. *Brian's Winter* describes what would have happened if Brian had not been rescued at the end of *Hatchet*. In *The River*, Brian re-enacts his north woods survival for the benefit of government researchers, with a series of fresh challenges. *Brian's Return* tells the story of Brian's need to revisit his experience as an older teen. The final book, *Brian's Hunt*, is the story of Brian's ultimate return to the wild after he realizes that he will never be comfortable in modern society. For readers who want to know how Paulsen drew upon his own experiences when writing the series, read *Guts: The True Stories Behind Hatchet and the Brian Books*.

Book Summary of *Hatchet*

Brian Robeson, heading to the Canadian north woods in a small plane to see his father, finds his first trip in a single-engine plane exciting at first. That excitement turns to terror when the captain, who has given Brian a bit of background about flying a plane, dies of a sudden heart attack. Brian manages to survive the crash landing, but the submerged plane leaves him without basic survival equipment—except for the hatchet clipped to his belt.

With no survival training, Brian begins the arduous tasks of finding food, shelter, and warmth. His challenges—mosquitoes, wild animals, hunger—are colored by his memories of his mother's secret relationship and his parents' resulting divorce. Gradually, Brian not only survives, but he also triumphs. His eventual rescue is met with a maturity and calm developed during his 54 days of solitude and personal growth.

Cross-Curricular Connection

This book can be used for social studies lessons or a unit on survival.

Possible Texts for Text Sets

- George, Jean Craighead. *My Side of the Mountain*. Puffin Books, 2001.
- George, Jean Craighead. *Julie of the Wolves*. HarperCollins, 1997.
- Hobbs, Will. *The Big Wander*. Atheneum Books for Young Readers, 2004.
- Hobbs, Will. *Far North*. HarperCollins, 2004.
- Long, Denise. *Survivor Kid: A Practical Guide to Wilderness Survival*. Chicago Review Press, 2011.

Name _____

Date _____

Pre-Reading Theme Thoughts

Directions: Read each of the statements in the first column. Decide if you agree or disagree with the statements. Record your opinion by marking an **X** in the Agree or Disagree box for each statement. Explain your choices in the fourth column. There are no right or wrong answers.

Statement	Agree	Disagree	Explain Your Answer
A child should never travel without a parent.			
I could figure out how to survive alone in the woods.			
Parents should never get divorced.			
People should not keep secrets.			

Vocabulary Overview

Ten key words from this section are provided below with definitions and sentences about how the words are used in the book. Choose one of the vocabulary activity sheets (pages 15 or 16) for students to complete as they read this section. Monitor students as they work to ensure the definitions they have found are accurate and relate to the text. Finally, discuss these important vocabulary words with students. If you think these words or other words in the section warrant more time devoted to them, there are suggestions in the introduction for other vocabulary activities (page 5).

Word	Definition	Sentence about Text
rudder (ch. 1)	moveable blade that can be moved to change a ship's or a plane's direction	The pilot sits with his feet on the **rudder** pedals.
slewed (ch. 1)	slid uncontrollably	The plane **slews** to the right when Brian takes the controls.
tundra (ch. 1)	a vast, treeless stretch of frozen land	Brian's father works in the oil fields of Canada, where the forests end and the **tundra** begins.
wincing (ch. 1)	slightly grimacing	Brian notices the pilot **wincing** in pain and thinks it must be from indigestion.
turbulence (ch. 2)	sudden, violent movement of air	The plane bumps up and down when it hits **turbulence**.
transmitter (ch. 2)	machine that sends out radio signals	Brian tries to use the radio **transmitter** to call for help.
vague (ch. 2)	unclear	Brian has a **vague** feeling that he should change the plane's direction.
visualize (ch. 2)	form a mental picture; imagine	Brian tries to **visualize** what will happen if the plane hits the water.
keening (ch. 4)	sharp or piercing	Brian has a **keening** headache from an injury to his forehead.
remnants (ch. 4)	bits and pieces	Brian's windbreaker gets caught when he escapes the plane and is torn into **remnants**.

Name _____

Date _____

Understanding Vocabulary Words

Directions: The following words appear in this section of the book. Use context clues and reference materials to determine an accurate definition for each word.

Word	Definition
rudder (ch. 1)	
slewed (ch. 1)	
tundra (ch. 1)	
wincing (ch. 1)	
turbulence (ch. 2)	
transmitter (ch. 2)	
vague (ch. 2)	
visualize (ch. 2)	
keening (ch. 4)	
remnants (ch. 4)	

Name _____

Date _____

During-Reading Vocabulary Activity

Directions: As you read these chapters, record at least eight important words on the lines below. Try to find interesting, difficult, intriguing, special, or funny words. Your words can be long or short. They can be hard or easy to spell. After each word, use context clues in the text and reference materials to define the word.

- _____
- _____
- _____
- _____
- _____
- _____
- _____
- _____
- _____

Directions: Respond to these questions about the words in this section.

1. What **procedure** does Brian think about while he is waiting for the plane to run out of gas?

_____

_____

2. Why does Brian feel **desperation** about his situation?

_____

_____

Analyzing the Literature

Provided below are discussion questions you can use in small groups, with the whole class, or for written assignments. Each question is given at two levels so you can choose the right question for each group of students. Activity sheets with these questions are provided (pages 18–19) if you want students to write their responses. For each question, a few key discussion points are provided for your reference.

Story Element	■ Level 1	▲ Level 2	Key Discussion Points
Plot	What triggers the crisis in the first part of the story?	What event sets up the plot of the story? Why is this event critical?	The pilot's sudden death sets in motion a series of life and death challenges for Brian: setting the plane down, escaping the plane, and whatever might follow.
Setting	Where does Brian end up after he escapes from the plane? What would being there be like?	Discuss the role of the setting as it relates to the plot. Do you think the setting will help Brian or make things worse for him?	The northern woods are remote and relatively unpopulated. It will be unlikely for Brian to be found or to get help easily. The woods are bursting with animal life and vegetation. This could be seen as either helpful or frightening to Brian.
Character	What does Brian do while the plane is crashing?	What knowledge and skills does Brian draw upon as the plane is crashing? What does that tell you about him as a person?	Discuss how Brian thinks about what little he knows about planes. He tries to stay calm and works at problem solving. If time allows, ask students how they think they'd react in a similar crisis.
Plot	What is the unexpected challenge that Brian faces as the sun comes up after the crash?	Why do you think the author gives Brian the challenge of enduring swarms of mosquitoes after the crash?	The mosquitoes make things harder for Brian, making him feel panicked and like he has hit bottom. If time allows, discuss how he realizes that he is both lucky and unlucky. He's alive, but he's alone, scared, and in pain.

Name _____

Date _____

■ Analyzing the Literature

Directions: Think about the section you just read. Read each question and provide a response that includes textual evidence.

1. What triggers the crisis in the first part of the story?

    _____

    _____

    _____

    _____

2. Where does Brian end up after he escapes from the plane? What would being there be like?

    _____

    _____

    _____

    _____

3. What does Brian do while the plane is crashing?

    _____

    _____

    _____

    _____

4. What is the unexpected challenge that Brian faces as the sun comes up after the crash?

    _____

    _____

    _____

Name _____

Date _____

▲ Analyzing the Literature

Directions: Think about the section you just read. Read each question and provide a response that includes textual evidence.

1. What event sets up the plot of the story? Why is this event critical?

   _____

   _____

   _____

   _____

2. Discuss the role of the setting as it relates to the plot. Do you think the setting will help Brian or make things worse for him?

   _____

   _____

   _____

   _____

3. What knowledge and skills does Brian draw upon as the plane is crashing? What does that tell you about him as a person?

   _____

   _____

   _____

   _____

4. Why do you think the author gives Brian the challenge of enduring swarms of mosquitoes after the crash?

   _____

   _____

   _____

Name _____

Date _____

Reader Response

Directions: Choose one of the following prompts about this section to answer. Be sure you include a topic sentence in your response, use textual evidence to support your opinion, and provide a strong conclusion that summarizes your opinion.

Writing Prompts

- **Narrative Piece**—Brian handles the plane crash in a very mature way. Describe a time when you dealt with a crisis in your life. Were you as calm and collected as Brian?
- **Informative/Explanatory Piece**—Explain the steps that Brian takes to try to survive the plane crash. How might his talent for logical thinking help him survive in the forest?

_____

_____

_____

_____

_____

_____

_____

_____

_____

_____

_____

_____

_____

_____

Name _____

Date _____

Close Reading the Literature

Directions: Closely reread the last three paragraphs in chapter 3. Start with, "Then a wild crashing sound, ..." Stop with, "Nothing." Read each question and then revisit the text to find evidence that supports your answer.

1. Use details from the text to describe the plane's final landing in the lake. How does the plane move?

    _____

    _____

    _____

2. What does Brian do as the plane dives into the water? Give examples from the text.

    _____

    _____

    _____

3. Find evidence to support your conclusion about whether Brian knows what he is doing after the plane goes under the water.

    _____

    _____

    _____

4. The section ends with this single word: *Nothing*. Based on your reading of the text, what happens to Brian just before he "spirals into nothing"?

    _____

    _____

    _____

Name _____

Date _____

Making Connections–Parachute Design

Materials

- sheet of plastic or lightweight cloth
- marker
- round object to trace around, such as a large plate or a pan lid
- scissors
- masking tape
- hole punch
- four pieces of string, each eight inches long
- an object that can be tied onto the parachute (action figure, small toy, a large clip, etc.)

Procedure

1. Trace around the round object on the sheet of plastic or cloth. Cut out the circle.
2. Mark four evenly spaced spots around the edge of the circle.
3. Put a small square of tape over each of the marked spots. Punch holes through the tape.
4. Tie the ends of the strings through the punched holes.
5. Tie the other ends of the strings to the object.
6. Drop the parachute from a high place.

Response

1. Experiment with larger pieces of cloth, heavier objects, and longer pieces of string. What is the best combination?

_____

_____

_____

2. Based on the events in the story, do you think having a parachute would have helped Brian? If so, how?

_____

_____

_____

Name _____

Date _____

Creating with the Story Elements

Directions: Thinking about the story elements of character, setting, and plot in a novel is very important to understanding what is happening and why. Complete **one** of the following activities based on what you've read so far. Be creative, and have fun!

Characters

Rate the pilot's performance on a scale of 1 (low) to 5 (high). Think about his actions before his death. Does he do anything that helps Brian? Explain your rating.

Setting

Refer to the descriptions of the setting in chapters 3 and 4. Visualize what the setting would look like as seen from the plane. Create a drawing or a three-dimensional model that presents the bird's-eye view of this setting.

Plot

Brian has a hatchet attached to his belt. What would you put on your belt or in your pockets if you knew you were going to be in an emergency? Brainstorm a list of at least ten items that would be useful to have, such as a cell phone, batteries, food, matches, and a first aid kit. Then limit your choices to five items that you could fit in your pockets. Justify your choices.

Vocabulary Overview

Ten key words from this section are provided below with definitions and sentences about how the words are used in the book. Choose one of the vocabulary activity sheets (pages 25 or 26) for students to complete as they read this section. Monitor students as they work to ensure the definitions they have found are accurate and relate to the text. Finally, discuss these important vocabulary words with students. If you think these words or other words in the section warrant more time devoted to them, there are suggestions in the introduction for other vocabulary activities (page 5).

Word	Definition	Sentence about Text
frantic (ch. 5)	desperate with fear or worry	Brian's parents will be **frantic** with worry when they learn of his disappearance.
extensive (ch. 5)	widespread	After a plane crash, there is usually an **extensive** search for survivors.
amphibious (ch. 5)	suited to both land and water	An **amphibious** plane is helpful for forest rescues because it can land on water.
diminish (ch. 6)	lessen	Brian doesn't want to **diminish** his chance to be found. So he stays near the lake.
pulverized (ch. 6)	crushed into tiny particles	A glacier has **pulverized** part of the rocks into sand.
watertight (ch. 6)	sealed so that no water can get in or out	The rock overhang creates a natural **watertight** roof for Brian.
driftwood (ch. 6)	wood that has floated ashore	Brian sees **driftwood** and branches everywhere, but he does not know how to start a fire.
interlaced (ch. 6)	woven together	Brian weaves together branches to make an **interlaced** wall for his shelter.
gorge (ch. 7)	eat too much	Brian smartly knows not to **gorge** on the raspberries, even though he is very hungry.
rivulets (ch. 7)	small streams of water	From his dry shelter, Brian watches the pouring rain make **rivulets** into the lake.

Name _____

Date _____

Understanding Vocabulary Words

Directions: The following words appear in this section of the book. Use context clues and reference materials to determine an accurate definition for each word.

Word	Definition
frantic (ch. 5)	
extensive (ch. 5)	
amphibious (ch. 5)	
diminish (ch. 6)	
pulverized (ch. 6)	
watertight (ch. 6)	
driftwood (ch. 6)	
interlaced (ch. 6)	
gorge (ch. 7)	
rivulets (ch. 7)	

Name _____

Date _____

During-Reading Vocabulary Activity

Directions: As you read these chapters, record at least eight important words on the lines below. Try to find interesting, difficult, intriguing, special, or funny words. Your words can be long or short. They can be hard or easy to spell. After each word, use context clues in the text and reference materials to define the word.

- _____
- _____
- _____
- _____
- _____
- _____
- _____
- _____
- _____
- _____

Directions: Respond to these questions about the words in this section.

1. What **assets** does Brian have as he works to survive being alone in the wilderness?

_____

_____

2. What things cause **frustration** for Brian during his first few days on his own?

_____

_____

Analyzing the Literature

Provided below are discussion questions you can use in small groups, with the whole class, or for written assignments. Each question is given at two levels so you can choose the right question for each group of students. Activity sheets with these questions are provided (pages 28–29) if you want students to write their responses. For each question, a few key discussion points are provided for your reference.

Story Element	■ Level 1	▲ Level 2	Key Discussion Points
Character	Brian wishes his friend Terry were with him. How might that have helped?	Brian and his friend Terry once pretended to be lost in the woods. How can pretending be useful?	It is comforting to have a friend with you in scary situations. Terry also could have helped Brian with solving problems, building a shelter, etc. Because the boys had previously pretended to be in a survival situation, Brian already had some thoughts about ways to improve his situation.
Plot	What developments might make it less likely that Brian will be rescued?	Why is it unlikely that Brian will be rescued in the immediate future? What impact does that have on Brian?	The plane jerked off course when the pilot became ill. It then flew for many hours in an unplanned direction. Brian realizes he has to figure out how to survive on his own without an immediate rescue.
Setting	How do the birds help Brian find food? What happens after he eats so much?	What role do the berries play in Brian's ability to cope at first?	Brian sees 20 or 30 birds land on one tree and realizes that they are eating berries. After eating, Brian feels like he can get to work and do more because he has had some food. He feels more confident. Later, however, the berries make him ill.
Character	Why is Brian upset with his mother?	Why wouldn't Brian want Terry to see his mother with the man?	Brian sees his mother kissing a man who isn't Brian's father. He is upset and ashamed that his friend might find out about his mother's actions.

Name _____

Date _____

Analyzing the Literature

Directions: Think about the section you just read. Read each question and provide a response that includes textual evidence.

1. Brian wishes his friend Terry were with him. How might that have helped?

_____

_____

_____

_____

2. What developments might make it less likely that Brian will be rescued?

_____

_____

_____

_____

3. How do the birds help Brian find food? What happens after he eats so much?

_____

_____

_____

_____

4. Why is Brian upset with his mother?

_____

_____

_____

_____

Name _____

Date _____

▲ Analyzing the Literature

Directions: Think about the section you just read. Read each question and provide a response that includes textual evidence.

1. Brian and his friend Terry once pretended to be lost in the woods. How can pretending be useful?

_____

_____

_____

_____

2. Why is it unlikely that Brian will be rescued in the immediate future? What impact does that have on Brian?

_____

_____

_____

_____

3. What role do the berries play in Brian's ability to cope at first?

_____

_____

_____

_____

4. Why wouldn't Brian want Terry to see his mother with the man?

_____

_____

_____

Name _____

Date _____

Reader Response

Directions: Choose one of the following prompts about this section to answer. Be sure you include a topic sentence in your response, use textual evidence to support your opinion, and provide a strong conclusion that summarizes your opinion.

Writing Prompts

- **Narrative Piece**—What advice would you like to be able to give Brian in this chapter? Have you learned anything from your life experiences that might help him?
- **Opinion/Argument Piece**—Why do you think Gary Paulsen chose to have Brian be alone for the crash? How might the story be different if Brian had someone with him?

_____

_____

_____

_____

_____

_____

_____

_____

_____

_____

_____

_____

_____

Name _____

Date _____

Close Reading the Literature

Directions: Closely reread the last seven paragraphs of chapter 8. Begin with, "The nick wasn't too large, ..." Read each question, and then revisit the text to find evidence that supports your answer.

1. What details from the text tell you that Brian shouldn't have thrown his hatchet?

   _____

   _____

   _____

2. What is the purpose of the dreams Brian has about his father and about Terry? What clues in the text tell you this?

   _____

   _____

   _____

3. Use specifics from the book to explain how Brian first starts to use his hatchet.

   _____

   _____

   _____

4. What event in this section brings a lot of relief to Brian? Why does he smile about what happened?

   _____

   _____

   _____

   _____

Name _____

Date _____

Making Connections–Facing the Future

Think about Brian's personality. Is he thoughtful? Impulsive? Determined? Patient? Some characteristics have both positive (pro) and negative (con) sides. For example, some kids wait until the last minute to do their homework. That can make it hard to get the work done on time, but that pressure can also help a person concentrate.

Directions: Think about Brian's personality. Choose three personality traits you think he exhibits. Explain how each trait has a pro and a con side.

Personality Trait	
Pro Side	**Con Side**

Personality Trait	
Pro Side	**Con Side**

Personality Trait	
Pro Side	**Con Side**

1. Share a sentence or two from the story that describes the personality trait you think will be the most helpful to Brian in the wilderness.

_____

_____

_____

_____

Name _____

Date _____

Creating with the Story Elements

Directions: Thinking about the story elements of character, setting, and plot in a novel is very important to understanding what is happening and why. Complete **one** of the following activities based on what you've read so far. Be creative and have fun!

Characters

Write a character profile. Your character should be someone who is perfectly suited to survive in the wilderness. Think about what attributes and traits would be most helpful for someone in that situation. Write at least five sentences that describe your character.

Setting

What are the scariest things about the setting? List at least five things found in the setting. They could be things such as the lake or the animals. Rank each one on a scale from 1 (least scary) to 5 (most scary). Then describe why you would **not** want to face the scariest thing on your list.

Plot

Recreate this consequences chart. Choose a decision that Brian makes. Describe the choice he makes and the resulting consequence. Then, describe a different choice he could have made in that same situation. Explain how the consequence would then have been different.

Decision *(include page number)*	
Choice	**Different Choice**
↓	↓
Consequence	New Consequence

Vocabulary Overview

Ten key words from this section are provided below with definitions and sentences about how the words are used in the book. Choose one of the vocabulary activity sheets (pages 35 or 36) for students to complete as they read this section. Monitor students as they work to ensure the definitions they have found are accurate and relate to the text. Finally, discuss these important vocabulary words with students. If you think these words or other words in the section warrant more time devoted to them, there are suggestions in the introduction for other vocabulary activities (page 5).

Word	Definition	Sentence about Text
ignite (ch. 9)	catch fire	Brian needs to find a material that will **ignite** when sparks hit it.
flue (ch. 9)	a pipe that carries smoke away from a fire	The rocks create a natural **flue** that carries smoke up through the roof.
regulate (ch. 10)	control	Brian needs to **regulate** his sleep so that he can wake up often and keep his fire going.
convulse (ch. 10)	shake or shudder violently	The taste of the greasy turtle egg makes Brian **convulse** in disgust.
literally (ch. 10)	meaning exactly what you say	Brian has to **literally** turn away from the eggs so he can keep himself from eating more of them.
transferred (ch. 11)	moved from one place to another	The only way to keep the eggs safe is to **transfer** them to the shelter and hide them.
signal (ch. 11)	something that acts as an indicator or a warning	Brian wants to have a **signal** fire ready in case a plane comes looking for him.
flailing (ch. 12)	swinging wildly	When Brian first starts fishing, he tries everything but **flailing** with his spear.
lunging (ch. 12)	making a quick forward movement	**Lunging** at the fish with the spear doesn't work.
persistent (ch. 12)	continuing; refusing to give up	Brian hears a **persistent** whine but doesn't realize right away that it is a plane motor.

Name _____

Date _____

Understanding Vocabulary Words

Directions: The following words appear in this section of the book. Use context clues and reference materials to determine an accurate definition for each word.

Word	Definition
ignite (ch. 9)	
flue (ch. 9)	
regulate (ch. 10)	
convulse (ch. 10)	
literally (ch. 10)	
transferred (ch. 11)	
signal (ch. 11)	
flailing (ch. 12)	
lunging (ch. 12)	
persistent (ch. 12)	

Name _____

Date _____

During-Reading Vocabulary Activity

Directions: As you read these chapters, record at least eight important words on the lines below. Try to find interesting, difficult, intriguing, special, or funny words. Your words can be long or short. They can be hard or easy to spell. After each word, use context clues in the text and reference materials to define the word.

- _____
- _____
- _____
- _____
- _____
- _____
- _____
- _____
- _____
- _____

Directions: Now, organize your words. Rewrite each of your words on a sticky note. Work as a group to create a bar graph of your words. You should stack any words that are the same on top of one another. Different words appear in different columns. Finally, discuss with a group why certain words were chosen more often than other words.

Analyzing the Literature

Provided below are discussion questions you can use in small groups, with the whole class, or for written assignments. Each question is given at two levels so you can choose the right question for each group of students. Activity sheets with these questions are provided (pages 38–39) if you want students to write their responses. For each question, a few key discussion points are provided for your reference.

Story Element	■ Level 1	▲ Level 2	Key Discussion Points
Plot	Why is making a fire so important to Brian?	Describe the benefits Brian gets from the fire.	Brian has a source of heat and a way of cooking food should he find it. He discovers that fire keeps the mosquitoes away. It can also be used to signal planes. Creating fire gives him feelings of hope and success.
Plot	Why do you think Gary Paulsen named the book *Hatchet*?	Why is the hatchet important to the plot? What other titles might Paulsen have used for the book? Would they be as powerful?	Discuss the role of the hatchet in Brian's survival so far. If time allows, draw attention to the foreshadowing of its importance when Brian's mother attaches it to his belt. Title options vary, but could include *Crashed!*, *Surviving*, or *Alone in the Wilderness*.
Setting	Why doesn't the search plane find Brian?	What could Brian have done to have a better chance of being seen by the searchers in the plane?	Brian's signal fire doesn't light fast enough, and the trees are tall, blocking the line of sight. Brian could have cleared an area and used rocks or branches to write the word help. He could have kept a signal fire going, although that would be difficult.
Character	How does Brian feel at the end of chapter 12? What might he do next?	At the end of chapter 12, Brian feels hopeless. Why does he feel like this is a game with nothing left for him? What would you do next?	Brian is working hard, but he is thinking in the short term. He thinks he will be found soon. When the plane flies off, Brian's expectations change. He no longer hopes for a quick rescue. He could react to this by giving up or by starting to work for long-term survival.

Name _____

Date _____

■ Analyzing the Literature

Directions: Think about the section you just read. Read each question and provide a response that includes textual evidence.

1. Why is making a fire so important to Brian?

_____

_____

_____

_____

2. Why do you think Gary Paulsen named the book *Hatchet*?

_____

_____

_____

_____

3. Why doesn't the search plane find Brian?

_____

_____

_____

_____

4. How does Brian feel at the end of chapter 12? What might he do next?

_____

_____

_____

_____

Name _____

Date _____

▲ Analyzing the Literature

Directions: Think about the section you just read. Read each question and provide a response that includes textual evidence.

1. Describe the benefits Brian gets from the fire.

   _____

   _____

   _____

   _____

2. Why is the hatchet important to the plot. What other titles might Paulsen have used for the book? Would they be as powerful?

   _____

   _____

   _____

   _____

3. What could Brian have done to have a better chance of being seen by the searchers in the plane?

   _____

   _____

   _____

   _____

4. At the end of chapter 12, Brian feels hopeless. Why does he feel like this is a game with nothing left for him? What would you do next?

   _____

   _____

   _____

Name _____

Date _____

Reader Response

Directions: Choose one of the following prompts about this section to answer. Be sure you include a topic sentence in your response, use textual evidence to support your opinion, and provide a strong conclusion that summarizes your opinion.

Writing Prompts

- **Informative/Explanatory Piece**—Explain in detail Brian's setback at the end of chapter 12. Then, describe what advice you would give him to help him persevere.
- **Opinion/Argument Piece**—For what reasons does Gary Paulsen have a search airplane pass over but not find Brian at this point in the book?

_____
_____
_____
_____
_____
_____
_____
_____
_____
_____
_____
_____
_____
_____

Name _____

Date _____

Close Reading the Literature

Directions: Closely reread the section in the middle of chapter 11 that begins with, "At the last trip to the top . . . ." Read through the paragraph that begins with, "He had no hooks or string . . . ." Read each question, and then revisit the text to find evidence that supports your answer.

1. Describe how Brian feels about his environment when he views it from atop of the rocks. What tells you that Brian has both positive and negative feelings about the area in which he is living?

   _____

   _____

   _____

2. Describe what Brian sees that gives him an idea about how to get some food?

   _____

   _____

   _____

3. What specific words in this section help the author describe what Brian discovers in the lake?

   _____

   _____

   _____

4. Brian does not have any fishing gear. What evidence in the text tells you that Brian has hope that he can catch fish anyway?

   _____

   _____

   _____

Name _____

Date _____

Making Connections–Making Plans

Directions: In these chapters, Brian realizes he has "things to do." Plan five days of work for Brian. Think about needs such as food, shelter, water, and sleep. Plan for both day-to-day needs and long-term needs. Write the suggested activities in the chart below.

	Day 1	Day 2	Day 3	Day 4	Day 5
Early Morning					
Morning					
Afternoon					
Early Evening					
Evening					

Name _____

Date _____

Creating with the Story Elements

Directions: Thinking about the story elements of character, setting, and plot in a novel is very important to understanding what is happening and why. Complete **one** of the following activities based on what you've read so far. Be creative and have fun!

Characters

The role of the hatchet in this story is almost as important as that of a live character. Create a poster advertisement for Brian's hatchet. List all its good qualities. Include its potential usefulness when trying to survive in the wilderness.

Setting

The setting in the woods has many positive and negative aspects for Brian. Make a T-chart that lists things that are good about being alone in the woods and things that are bad.

Plot

In *Hatchet,* the story develops from Brian's point of view. Write a plot outline of what you imagine is happening in the meantime with either Brian's mother or his father.

Vocabulary Overview

Ten key words from this section are provided below with definitions and sentences about how the words are used in the book. Choose one of the vocabulary activity sheets (pages 45 or 46) for students to complete as they read this section. Monitor students as they work to ensure the definitions they have found are accurate and relate to the text. Finally, discuss these important vocabulary words with students. If you think these words or other words in the section warrant more time devoted to them, there are suggestions in the introduction for other vocabulary activities (page 5).

Word	Definition	Sentence about Text
tension (ch. 13)	being strained or held tight	Brian relaxes the **tension** on the spear when he decides the wolf is not a threat to him.
infuriating (ch. 13)	making someone furious	It is **infuriating** to not be able to spear the fish.
fashioned (ch. 13)	made into a particular form	Brian **fashions** the arrows by himself.
rectify (ch. 14)	correct	In the woods, there often isn't a way to **rectify** your mistakes.
vital (ch. 14)	essential	Brian knows that the most **vital** objective in the forest is the search for food.
impaired (ch. 14)	damaged	After the skunk sprays Brian in the eyes, he fears his eyesight is **impaired** forever.
weave (ch. 14)	interlace pieces together	Brian **weaves** together long branches and thinner ones to make a wall for his shelter.
relatively (ch. 14)	in comparison to something else	Brian feels **relatively** safe after he creates a door for his shelter.
camouflage (ch. 15)	disguise	The foolbirds' **camouflage** makes them almost impossible to see.
stabilize (ch. 15)	to make steady	The arrows will not fly straight because they have no feathers attached to **stabilize** them.

Name _____

Date _____

Understanding Vocabulary Words

Directions: The following words appear in this section of the book. Use context clues and reference materials to determine an accurate definition for each word.

Word	Definition
tension (ch. 13)	
infuriating (ch. 13)	
fashioned (ch. 13)	
rectify (ch. 14)	
vital (ch. 14)	
impaired (ch. 14)	
weave (ch. 14)	
relatively (ch. 14)	
camouflage (ch. 15)	
stabilize (ch. 15)	

Name _____

Date _____

During-Reading Vocabulary Activity

Directions: As you read these chapters, record at least eight important words on the lines below. Try to find interesting, difficult, intriguing, special, or funny words. Your words can be long or short. They can be hard or easy to spell. After each word, use context clues in the text and reference materials to define the word.

- _____
- _____
- _____
- _____
- _____
- _____
- _____
- _____
- _____

Directions: Respond to these questions about the words in this section.

1. How does Brian **exult** when he finally succeeds with the bow and arrow?

_____

_____

2. What are some examples of ways Brian shows **patience** as he fights to survive?

_____

_____

Analyzing the Literature

Provided below are discussion questions you can use in small groups, with the whole class, or for written assignments. Each question is given at two levels so you can choose the right question for each group of students. Activity sheets with these questions are provided (pages 48–49) if you want students to write their responses. For each question, a few key discussion points are provided for your reference.

Story Element	■ Level 1	▲ Level 2	Key Discussion Points
Plot	What does Brian need to remember about light and water to fish successfully?	What is the solution to the problem Brian has of catching fish?	Brian remembers that water refracts light. Things in water appear to bend. He adjusts his aim to account for this, finally catching a fish.
Character	In chapter 13, Brian remembers a time 42 days earlier when he wanted to die. Why did he feel that way?	Contrast Brian's feelings before the plane appears and after it passes overhead.	Discuss Brian's desperation at not being rescued, how he hits bottom and could easily have given up and died. Then discuss how Brian recovers and becomes a tougher, more resilient person.
Character	What does Brian mean, at the end of chapter 13, when he says he is full of tough hope?	Describe how Brian's view of hope evolves.	At first, Brian holds out hope that he will be rescued. After the plane passes overhead, he loses that hope. But soon he finds a new optimism building within. He has hope that he can learn to take care of himself and survive alone.
Setting	What does Brian learn from the encounter with the skunk?	How does Brian change his behavior after the skunk sprays him?	Brian realizes he must become more proactive in his thinking. He improves his shelter. He wants it to keep him safe and not just protect him from wind and rain. He also works to make a safe place where he can store food for the future.

Name _____

Date _____

■ Analyzing the Literature

Directions: Think about the section you just read. Read each question and provide a response that includes textual evidence.

1. What does Brian need to remember about light and water to fish successfully?

   _____

   _____

   _____

   _____

2. In chapter 13, Brian remembers a time 42 days earlier when he wanted to die. Why did he feel that way?

   _____

   _____

   _____

   _____

3. What does Brian mean, at the end of chapter 13, when he says he is full of tough hope?

   _____

   _____

   _____

   _____

4. What does Brian learn from the encounter with the skunk?

   _____

   _____

   _____

Name _____

Date _____

▲ Analyzing the Literature

Directions: Think about the section you just read. Read each question and provide a response that includes textual evidence.

1. What is the solution to the problem Brian has of catching fish?

    _____

    _____

    _____

    _____

2. Contrast Brian's feelings before the plane appears and after it passes overhead.

    _____

    _____

    _____

    _____

3. Describe how Brian's view of hope evolves.

    _____

    _____

    _____

    _____

4. How does Brian change his behavior after the skunk sprays him?

    _____

    _____

    _____

    _____

Name _____

Date _____

Reader Response

Directions: Choose one of the following prompts about this section to answer. Be sure you include a topic sentence in your response, use textual evidence to support your opinion, and provide a strong conclusion that summarizes your opinion.

Writing Prompts

- **Opinion/Argument Piece**—If you were in Brian's shoes, which event do you think would be more devastating: the attack by the moose or the tornado? Be sure to include details from the story to support your argument.
- **Narrative Piece**—Make connections between this section of the book and earlier sections. Describe how Brian's outlook has changed as he is forced to continue surviving alone.

_____

_____

_____

_____

_____

_____

_____

_____

_____

_____

_____

_____

_____

_____

Name _____

Date _____

Close Reading the Literature

Directions: Closely reread the first seven paragraphs in chapter 15. Read each question and then revisit the text to find evidence that supports your answer.

1. Use details from the text to describe the difference between how Brian tracks days and how he tracks important events.

   _____

   _____

   _____

2. What specific incident leaves Brian intent on getting meat to eat? Include details about what he experiences.

   _____

   _____

   _____

3. Brian thinks he might be able to shoot a rabbit but not a squirrel. Use information from the text to contrast his descriptions of the two animals and explain why he thinks this.

   _____

   _____

   _____

4. What exactly about the foolbirds frustrates Brian?

   _____

   _____

   _____

   _____

Name _____

Date _____

Making Connections—Lost in Paradise

Directions: Imagine two very different settings, the northern woods and a deserted island. Think about how they are similar and different. Four categories are listed below. Add two more. Then compare the two settings. Use the Internet or other resources for additional information, if necessary.

Features	Northern Woods	Deserted Island
Food sources		
Water sources		
Animals		
Possible disasters		

1. If you were stranded alone, which setting would you prefer? Give evidence to support your choice.

   _____

   _____

   _____

   _____

Name _____

Date _____

Creating with the Story Elements

Directions: Thinking about the story elements of character, setting, and plot in a novel is very important to understanding what is happening and why. Complete **one** of the following activities based on what you've read so far. Be creative and have fun!

Characters

Recreate this chart. Choose three important characteristics about Brian. Use evidence from the book to make your choices. Write these in the first column. Write three important characteristics about you in the second column. Write how you and Brian are alike and different in the third column.

All About Brian	All About Me	How We Are Alike and Different

Setting

The setting is important in chapter 16. Brian compares his bad day to the flip of a giant coin. But there are two sides to every coin. Choose two key events from chapter 16. Write the bad news related to the event in one paragraph. Write the good news about the event in a second paragraph.

Plot

When little things add up and become significant enough to force a big change, it's called the *tipping point*. Brian's tipping point comes when he realizes that he truly can survive alone. Create an image that shows the little things that add up to Brian's tipping point. Label the small steps and his big change. They could be depicted on a path, on a graph, as if climbing a mountain, or any other creative illustration.

Vocabulary Overview

Ten key words from this section are provided below with definitions and sentences about how the words are used in the book. Choose one of the vocabulary activity sheets (pages 55 or 56) for students to complete as they read this section. Monitor students as they work to ensure the definitions they have found are accurate and relate to the text. Finally, discuss these important vocabulary words with students. If you think these words or other words in the section warrant more time devoted to them, there are suggestions in the introduction for other vocabulary activities (page 5).

Word	Definition	Sentence about Text
wreckage (ch. 17)	ruins	After the tornado, Brian looks at the **wreckage** of his campsite and knows he has work to do.
crudely (ch. 17)	roughly	The repairs to his shelter are done **crudely**, but they are enough for now.
crosspieces (ch. 17)	pieces that lie across a structure to stabilize it	Brian has trouble keeping his raft together because he has no **crosspieces** or fasteners.
momentary (ch. 17)	brief	Brian has a **momentary** loss of temper that makes him feel like his old self.
tattered (ch. 17)	ragged and torn	Brian tears up his **tattered** windbreaker and uses the strips to make a rope.
murky (ch. 17)	dark and gloomy	It is difficult for Brian to examine the plane because it sits in **murky** water.
stabilizer (ch. 18)	a part that steadies a plane	Brian tries to find a way into the plane alongside the **stabilizer**.
visibility (ch. 18)	view; what can be seen	There is little **visibility** under the water, making it hard for Brian to find his hatchet after he drops it.
capacity (ch. 18)	the amount that something can hold	Brian knows he has to dive deep to retrieve his hatchet, so he fills his lungs to their **capacity**.
substantial (ch. 18)	important in size or worth	At first, Brian finds nothing **substantial** inside the plane.

Name _____

Date _____

Understanding Vocabulary Words

Directions: The following words appear in this section of the book. Use context clues and reference materials to determine an accurate definition for each word.

Word	Definition
wreckage (ch. 17)	
crudely (ch. 17)	
crosspieces (ch. 17)	
momentary (ch. 17)	
tattered (ch. 17)	
murky (ch. 17)	
stabilizer (ch. 18)	
visibility (ch. 18)	
capacity (ch. 18)	
substantial (ch. 18)	

Name _____

Date _____

During-Reading Vocabulary Activity

Directions: As you read these chapters, choose five important words from the story. Use these words to complete the word flow chart below. On each arrow, write a word. In each box, explain how the connected pair of words relates to each other. An example for the words *murky* and *visibility* has been done for you.

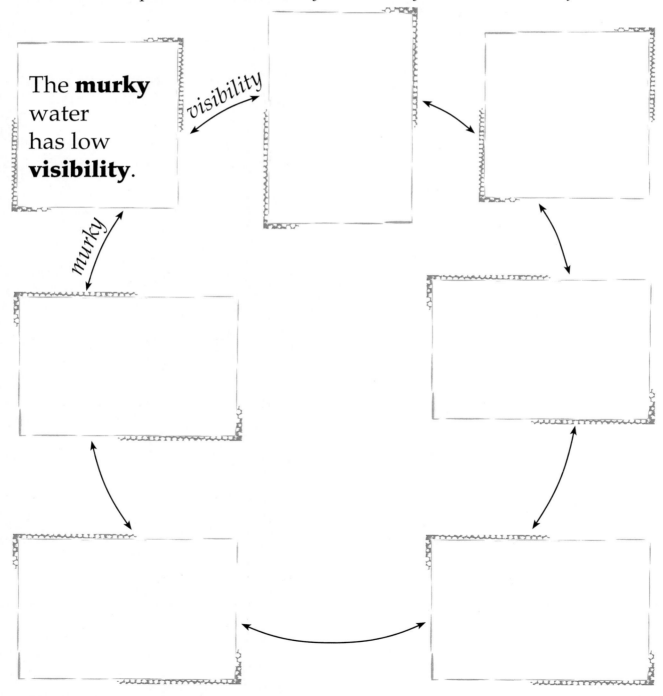

The **murky** water has low **visibility**.

visibility

murky

Analyzing the Literature

Provided below are discussion questions you can use in small groups, with the whole class, or for written assignments. Each question is given at two levels so you can choose the right question for each group of students. Activity sheets with these questions are provided (pages 58–59) if you want students to write their responses. For each question, a few key discussion points are provided for your reference.

Story Element	■ Level 1	▲ Level 2	Key Discussion Points
Plot	What jobs keep Brian busy right after the tornado?	Brian does a lot of unexciting jobs before he tries to get into the plane. Why is that wise?	After the tornado, Brian restarts his fire, rebuilds his shelter, and sets about getting more food and making new tools. Brian needs time to heal. He can also think about the challenges ahead while he is completing routine tasks.
Setting	What about the plane's location makes getting into it so difficult?	What role does the lake play in the plot after Brian drops his hatchet?	The plane is in the middle of the lake and partially under water. Brian has to build a raft to get there and then use his precious hatchet to hack through the aluminum covering of the plane. After he drops the hatchet, he has to dive for it, drawing upon more reserves of strength and endurance.
Character	What has happened to the dead pilot?	How does Brian react to the condition of the dead pilot?	The fish have eaten the pilot's flesh, leaving only a skull. Brian's reaction helps propel him to the surface. If time allows, discuss how terrible images can sometimes stay with a person, making it difficult for them later.
Plot	How does Brian react to the arrival of the rescue pilot?	Contrast Brian's reaction to the arrival of the rescue pilot with the reaction of the pilot when he sees Brian.	Brian is very calm, and he offers the pilot food. In contrast, the pilot is stunned at finding Brian after so long. If time allows, discuss how Brian had little time to adjust to the unexpected, sudden landing of the plane.

Name _____

Date _____

■ Analyzing the Literature

Directions: Think about the section you just read. Read each question and state your response with textual evidence.

1. What jobs keep Brian busy right after the tornado?

_____

_____

_____

_____

2. What about the plane's location makes getting into it so difficult?

_____

_____

_____

_____

3. What has happened to the dead pilot?

_____

_____

_____

_____

4. How does Brian react to the arrival of the rescue pilot?

_____

_____

_____

_____

Name _____

Date _____

▲ Analyzing the Literature

Directions: Think about the section you just read. Read each question and state your response with textual evidence.

1. Brian does a lot of unexciting jobs before he tries to get into the plane. Why is that wise?

   _____

   _____

   _____

   _____

2. What role does the lake play in the plot after Brian drops his hatchet?

   _____

   _____

   _____

   _____

3. How does Brian react to the condition of the dead pilot?

   _____

   _____

   _____

   _____

4. Contrast Brian's reaction to the arrival of the rescue pilot with the reaction of the pilot when he sees Brian.

   _____

   _____

   _____

   _____

Name _____

Date _____

Reader Response

Directions: Choose one of the following prompts about this section to answer. Be sure you include a topic sentence in your response, use textual evidence to support your opinion, and provide a strong conclusion that summarizes your opinion.

Writing Prompts

- **Opinion/Argument Piece**—Describe and explain why you would or would not like to go through an experience like Brian does. Use textual evidence from the story to explain your opinion.
- **Narrative Piece**—Gary Paulsen wrote several other novels about Brian. Before you read any of them, predict what you think will happen to Brian next. How will his life change because of what he goes through in *Hatchet*?

_____

_____

_____

_____

_____

_____

_____

_____

_____

_____

_____

_____

_____

_____

_____

Name _____

Date _____

Close Reading the Literature

Directions: Closely reread the first eight paragraphs in chapter 19, finishing with, ". . . he wasn't sure he liked the change." Read each question, and then revisit the text to find evidence that supports your answer.

1. Using evidence from the story, explain why Brian doesn't open the survival pack right away.

   _____

   _____

   _____

2. Describe at least five of the riches that Brian finds in the survival pack.

   _____

   _____

   _____

3. What is one example from this section that explains how survival is suddenly an easier prospect for Brian?

   _____

   _____

   _____

4. How does the author describe Brian's mixed feelings about two items from the survival pack?

   _____

   _____

   _____

   _____

Name _____

Date _____

Making Connections–What's Your Style?

Directions: Some people learn through trial and error. They like to experiment. Other people make a choice, plan a lot, and stick with it. Complete the inventory to show how you think Brian responds to challenges. Place an **X** on the line to show where he fits. Then, include evidence to justify your choices.

Brian gets input from many sources. ⟶	Brian relies on himself.
Evidence:	
Brian acts first and then thinks. ⟶	Brian thinks and then acts.
Evidence:	
Brian tries many solutions. ⟶	Brian makes one idea work.
Evidence:	
Brian takes lots of risks. ⟶	Brian takes few risks.
Evidence:	

Directions: Your turn! How would you respond to being lost in the woods? Rate your learning style. Explain each answer.

I get input from many sources. ⟶	I rely on myself.
Explain:	
I act first and then think. ⟶	I think and then act.
Explain:	
I try many solutions. ⟶	I make one idea work.
Explain:	
I take lots of risks. ⟶	I take few risks.
Explain:	

Name _____

Date _____

Creating with the Story Elements

Directions: Thinking about the story elements of character, setting, and plot in a novel is very important to understanding what is happening and why. Complete **one** of the following activities based on what you've read so far. Be creative and have fun!

Characters

Think about what Brian is like. Consider his talents, skills, and personality traits. Choose the top three things about him that make him unique. Rank them from one to three. Write a paragraph about each one and why each will be important to Brian when he is an adult.

Setting

Create a bird's-eye view of the setting as seen from the rescue plane at the end of the story. Include Brian's campsite, the wreckage, the forest, and so forth. Make a drawing or a 3-D version.

Plot

Create a time line that shows the significant events from the story, starting with Day 1 when Brian's plane crashes. End with Day 54, when Brian is rescued. Label the significant events, such as the days Brian keeps in his mental journal. (It is okay to guess at when some of the major events happened.)

Name _____

Date _____

Post-Reading Theme Thoughts

Directions: Read each of the statements in the first column. Think about Brian's perspective. From his point of view, decide if he would agree or disagree with each statement. Record his opinion by marking an **X** in either the Agree or Disagree box for each statement. Explain your choices in the fourth column by using evidence from the text.

Statement	Agree	Disagree	Explain Your Answer
A child should never travel without a parent.			
I could figure out how to survive alone in the woods.			
Parents should never get divorced.			
People should not keep secrets.			

Name _____

Date _____

Culminating Activity: Survival

Directions: Brian changes a great deal during the course of *Hatchet*. At times he says that he feels like he becomes a completely different person. Since Brian is so different, it may be hard for him to adapt back to normal life. Make a list of ten things you think will be difficult for Brian when he returns to civilization. Then, on another piece of paper, choose one item from your list and suggest a strategy Brian could use to make this real-life situation easier.

- _____

- _____

- _____

- _____

- _____

- _____

- _____

- _____

- _____

- _____

Name _____

Date _____

Culminating Activity: Survival (cont.)

Directions: Complete one of the following projects.

- Pretend you are going to interview Brian for a magazine article. Write a list of questions you want to ask. Come up with a variety of questions, adding questions about things that were *not* covered in the story. Include questions about what happens once Brian is home again. Your list should have at least 15 questions on it.

- Create a survival brochure or handbook. Think about the lessons Brian learned in the wilderness. Conduct additional research on the Internet or from other resources as necessary. Make sure the final product is organized and useful.

- The setting in the woods is the source of many problems for Brian. Complete the graphic organizer to describe how the setting affects Brian. One example is done for you. Choose one problem and write a paragraph to describe how Brian deals with it in the novel.

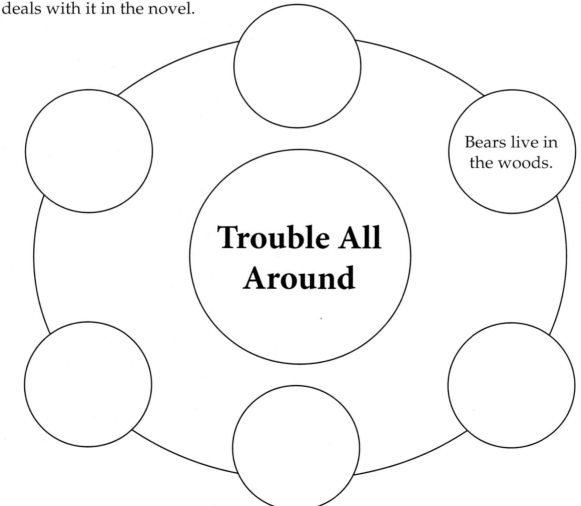

Trouble All Around

Bears live in the woods.

Name _____

Date _____

Comprehension Assessment

Directions: Circle the letter before the best response to each question.

1. What is the secret that Brian thinks about often?

    A. He doesn't know how to survive in the woods.

    B. He knows his parents will be worried about him.

    C. He saw his mother kissing a strange man.

    D. The pilot died in the crash.

2. Why is it unlikely that Brian will be rescued quickly?

    E. Brian has a hard time building a fire.

    F. The pilot probably dies of a heart attack.

    G. The plane goes off course before it crashes.

    H. Brian has to find food to eat first.

3. What is the main idea of this text?

    "Small mistakes could turn into disasters, funny little mistakes could snowball so that while you were still smiling at the humor you could find yourself looking at death. In the city if he made a mistake usually there was a way to rectify it, make it all right. If he fell on his bike and sprained a leg he could wait for it to heal; if he forgot something at the store he could find other food in the refrigerator."

    _____

    _____

    _____

    _____

4. Which **two** details together support your answer to question 3? Choose two answers.

    A. The survival pack contains many freeze-dried packages of food.

    B. The skunk steals Brian's eggs and sprays Brian in the eyes.

    C. Brian creates a food shelf above his shelter, to keep his food safe.

    D. When Brian returns home, he finds grocery stores overwhelming.

Comprehension Assessment (cont.)

5. Which statement best expresses one of the themes of the book?

    E. You should never tell a secret.

    F. Survival requires lots of patience and perseverance.

    G. Animals can be dangerous.

    H. Accidents can happen, so be prepared.

6. What quotation from the book provides the best evidence for your answer to number 5?

    A. "And that had been the secret."

    B. "Suddenly he could see things he never saw before."

    C. "Time and again, he drew, held, and let arrows fly . . . ."

    D. "And he had nearly smiled."

7. Explain the purpose of this sentence from the book: "The rifle changed him, the minute he picked it up, and he wasn't sure he liked the change very much."

    _____

    _____

    _____

    _____

    _____

8. Which other quotation from the story serves a purpose that is similar to the quotation in number 7?

    E. "He could deal with that feeling later."

    F. "It was like all the holidays in the world . . . ."

    G. "He had only a moment of warning."

    H. ". . . the lighter somehow removed him from where he was, what he had to know."

Response to Literature:
PowerPoint Presentation!

Directions: It's time to learn about nature and share with others! Follow these steps to create your own presentation.

- Choose an area where people can go hiking. You can choose somewhere close to where you live, or you can pick a well-known destination. Maybe you'd like to learn about Yellowstone National Park or Glacier National Park.

- Complete some basic research to discover more about the location you chose. You need to find out details about hiking in the area (weather, landforms, animals, etc.).

- Create a *PowerPoint* presentation that provides survival strategies for hiking in the area. Use the information you gathered in your research, and also include tips you learned by reading about Brian's struggle to survive in *Hatchet*. Include information about the following topics:
  - recommended trails and times of year to hike
  - recommended supplies for a hiker's backpack
  - recommended skills for a hiker
  - recommended personality traits in case a hiker gets lost
  - other key information

- Present your *PowerPoint* presentation to a classmate. Revise it as necessary before sharing with others.

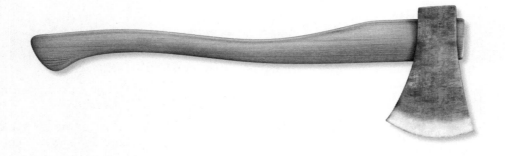

Name _____

Date _____

Response to Literature Rubric

Directions: Use this rubric to evaluate student responses.

	Exceptional Writing	Quality Writing	Developing Writing
Focus and Organization	☐ States a clear opinion and elaborates well. Engages the reader from the opening hook through the middle to the conclusion. Demonstrates clear understanding of the intended audience and purpose of the piece.	☐ Provides a clear and consistent opinion. Maintains a clear perspective and supports it through elaborating details. Makes the opinion clear in the opening hook and summarizes well in the conclusion.	☐ Provides an inconsistent point of view. Does not support the topic adequately or misses pertinent information. Provides lack of clarity in the beginning, middle, and conclusion.
Text Evidence	☐ Provides comprehensive and accurate support. Includes relevant and worthwhile text references.	☐ Provides limited support. Provides few supporting text references.	☐ Provides very limited support for the text. Provides no supporting text references.
Written Expression	☐ Uses descriptive and precise language with clarity and intention. Maintains a consistent voice and uses an appropriate tone that supports meaning. Uses multiple sentence types and transitions well between ideas.	☐ Uses a broad vocabulary. Maintains a consistent voice and supports a tone and feelings through language. Varies sentence length and word choices.	☐ Uses a limited and unvaried vocabulary. Provides an inconsistent or weak voice and tone. Provides little to no variation in sentence type and length.
Language Conventions	☐ Capitalizes, punctuates, and spells accurately. Demonstrates complete thoughts within sentences, with accurate subject-verb agreement. Uses paragraphs appropriately and with clear purpose.	☐ Capitalizes, punctuates, and spells accurately. Demonstrates complete thoughts within sentences and appropriate grammar. Paragraphs are properly divided and supported.	☐ Incorrectly capitalizes, punctuates, and spells. Uses fragmented or run-on sentences. Utilizes poor grammar overall. Paragraphs are poorly divided and developed.

The responses provided here are just examples of what students may answer. Many accurate responses are possible for the questions throughout this unit.

During-Reading Vocabulary Activity—Section 1: Chapters 1–4 (page 16)

1. Brian thinks about the **procedure** he will follow when the plane runs out of gas and starts to go down. He thinks about how to slow down the plane and what sort of terrain he should seek out.

2. Brian feels **desperation** because he doesn't know much about landing a plane, he can't get help on the radio, and he knows he is running out of time.

Close Reading the Literature—Section 1: Chapters 1–4 (page 21)

1. The plane rolls, blows through trees, skips on the water, and tears apart.

2. Brian is screaming, pulling at the seatbelt, and trying desperately to escape the plane.

3. Brian does not know what he is doing. He pulls at the weeds and muck. He swims without thinking, searching instinctively for safety.

4. Brian sees a color that he's never seen before. It explodes in his mind and he spirals into nothing. Brian loses consciousness from pain and shock.

During-Reading Vocabulary Activity—Section 2: Chapters 5–8 (page 26)

1. Brian's **assets** include being smart, having a hatchet, and knowing how to draw upon past experiences and knowledge.

2. Brian feels **frustration** at not being able to find food, start a fire, or get help. He feels as if he has nothing.

Close Reading the Literature—Section 2: Chapters 5–8 (page 31)

1. The hatchet is the only tool Brian has and is therefore vital. He feels remorse about having damaged it.

2. The dreams are telling Brian that the hatchet can be used to make fire because it makes sparks.

3. Brian strikes the stone with the back of the hatchet to make sparks.

4. Brian makes so many sparks that he knows he can make fire. He feels optimistic.

Close Reading the Literature—Section 3: Chapters 9–12 (page 41)

1. When Brian sees the lake from above he feels fear. Then he gets caught up in the beauty of the scenery, including the lake and the forest, which he describes as "a green carpet full of life."

2. Brian sees a kingfisher catching a fish and realizes the lake is full of fish.

3. Brian sees that the lake is "literally packed with life." He sees small fish everywhere, as well as clam shells and crayfish.

4. The fish are curious about Brian. They keep coming back, and there are many of them.

During-Reading Vocabulary Activity—Section 4: Chapters 13–16 (page 46)

1. Brian **exults** by holding the fish up to the sky and allowing himself a moment of pride and happiness.

2. Brian shows **patience** as he takes his time making his tools, catching fish and a bird, and cooking his food.

Close Reading the Literature—Section 4: Chapters 13–16 (page 51)

1. Brian makes a mark for each day on a stone near his shelter. But more important to him is the timing of certain events, which he records in a mental journal.

2. Brian craves meat. He dreams about his mother cooking meat and wakes one morning with saliva and the taste of pork chops in his mouth.

3. Brian thinks the squirrels are too small and fast to catch. He thinks he might be able to catch one of the bigger rabbits.

4. There are a lot of foolbirds, but he can't spot them, even when they are close. He can't figure out how to catch them because their camouflage is too good and they fly away before Brian even knows they are nearby.

Close Reading the Literature—Section 5: Chapters 17–Epilogue (page 61)

1. Brian is exhausted and needs to sleep after the hard work of swimming back from the plane and dragging the survival pack to his shelter.

2. He has a sleeping bag, a sleeping pad, a cookset, matches, lighters, a knife, a compass, a first-aid kit, scissors, a cap, a fishing kit, a rifle, soap, freeze-dried meals, and an emergency transmitter.

3. Brian could use a lighter to start a fire. Other possible answers are that he has more food, fishing equipment, a rifle for hunting, and/or a warm place to sleep.

4. Brian knows that the rifle and the lighter can make survival less difficult. But having these items makes him feel disconnected from his surroundings and his new knowledge. Brian isn't "sure he liked the change."

Comprehension Assessment (page 67–68)

1. C. He saw his mother kissing a strange man.

2. G. The plane goes off course before it crashes.

3. Main idea: One must be careful and learn from one's mistakes if one wants to survive in the wilderness.

4. Supporting details: B. The skunk steals Brian's eggs and sprays Brian in the eyes. C. Brian creates a food shelf above his shelter, to keep his food safe.

5. F. Survival requires lots of patience and perseverance.

6. C. "Time and again, he drew, held, and let arrows fly . . . ."

7. Possible answers include that he wasn't sure he wanted to be separated from the experience by shooting with a rifle, that he was uncomfortable with using a rifle, or that he preferred the learning that went with surviving without help from the rifle.

8. H. ". . . .the lighter somehow removed him from where he was, what he had to know."